D1609109

Hariri
&
Hariri
Houses

Hariri & Hariri Houses

Foreword by **Richard Meier**
Introduction by **Paul Goldberger**
Essay by **John Brehm**

728.37 Hariri c.1
Hariri & Hariri houses

30519007158986

RIZZOLI
NEW YORK

PROPERTY OF
HIGH POINT PUBLIC LIBRARY
HIGH POINT, NORTH CAROLINA

For Ava & Iman

First published in the United States of America in 2005 by
Rizzoli International Publications, Inc.
300 Park Avenue South
New York, NY 10010
www.rizzoliusa.com
© 2005 Rizzoli International Publications, Inc.

All rights reserved. No part of this publication may be reproduced, stored in a retrieval system, or transmitted in any form or by any means, electronic, mechanical, photocopying, recording, or otherwise, without prior consent of the publishers.

2005 2006 2007 2008 2009 / 10 9 8 7 6 5 4 3 2 1
ISBN: 0-8478-2779-8
ISBN 13: 978-0847827794
Library of Congress Catalog Control Number: 2005933795
Designed by Claudia Brandenburg, Language Arts
Printed in China

Foreword:
Richard Meier

The work of Gisue Hariri and Mojgan Hariri embodies a rare combination of minimal elegance and sensuality. Using a simple palette of materials—stone, glass, concrete, wood—they bring out the essence of each material. Even a rusted steel door takes on an unexpected elegance. Each detail is necessary, nothing is superfluous.

—

Their work is about creating space that is filled with light and pared down to its bare essentials. What does someone need to inhabit this space fully? A certain amount of openness, access to light, and views. By minimizing the distractions of decor and unnecessary complexities, one focuses on the elegance of the finish of the materials, on the balance of materials. There is a calming quality to the projects: these are contemplative spaces.

—

The house that the Hariris designed as part of the Houses at Sagaponac project beautifully captures the original spirit of the endeavor. The intention was to see if it was possible to recapture the attraction of many for the Hamptons—the ability to live simply, in touch with the beautiful nature of the area by creating houses that would be innovative and thoughtful in their design and modest in scale. The Sagaponac House that Hariri & Hariri has designed has an L-shaped configuration with all of the public spaces facing the interior courtyard and pool area, creating a communal outdoor living room. The simple, low, horizontal form of the house, clad in wood, hovers gently above the landscape. Here one is, again, in touch with the natural beauty and calm of the surroundings.

—

Their work successfully manages the balance between sculpture as pure form and inhabited space. Even when employing a very sculptural gesture, such as the folding planes in the Park Avenue Loft project, it is done with a purpose. In this case a fairly prosaic one—to hide lighting and wiring—but the result is far from prosaic. Rather, it is seamlessly woven into the overall organization of the space enlivening it with a play of rectilinear and curvilinear forms.

—

Given the often competing demands of program, budget, site, and client, it is difficult to maintain a focus on quality and basic principles, but Hariri and Hariri have done this with unwavering dedication. It is that dedication to quality, to paring things down to their essence, that gives the Hariris' work such depth and beauty and makes it such a joy to behold.

—

Preface:
Gisue Hariri

Architecture of Complementary Opposites

Sagaponac House

Where you are born and where you have lived is unimportant.
It is what you have done with where you have been that will be of interest.
—GEORGIA O'KEEFFE

Pound Ridge House

Growing up in Iran, my sister Mojgan and I were subject to distinct, severe, and clearly reinforced boundaries between men and women, private and public, inside and outside, interior and exterior. These thresholds existed in the architecture of cities, homes, public buildings, clothing, everything. Such separations created interesting structures, beautiful walls, mysterious alleyways, and hidden spaces. It was only after we began studying architecture at Cornell University, however, that we came to understand and value the open plan and the transparency and flexibility of modern architecture in the West. Our experience of living in these two profoundly different architectural environments allowed us to see what was missing from both and inspired us to bring together the best of each as complementary opposites. Our goal has been to create structures that blur the distinction between inside and outside, open and closed, private and public, visible and invisible, expected and unexpected.

The Digital House

The projects that resulted from this fusion simultaneously reject and accept the past and future. They are free from preconceived notions of style, formality, tradition, and hierarchy. These houses are about the experience of a place, of light, space, form, and material. They are dynamic yet peaceful, glamorous yet down-to-earth. They use state-of-the-art technology but do not lose sight of the poetry of life that we all carry within us.

Villa The Hague

Our inspirations for the design of these residential projects come from a variety of sources and places. We are inspired by art, poetry, a rock formation on the site, or movements of boats on a canal, a hologram, a pattern of markings on the bark of a tree, a Japanese garden, or a lantern. And we are equally interested in cutting-edge technology, prefabrication, and virtual reality. The variety of these sources of inspiration are perhaps best understood in relation to specific projects. For instance, with Barry's Bay Cottage, we were fascinated by the field of extremely tall birch trees that were on the property and which we wanted to keep. On our first visit to the site, the silvery skin of the birch trees was peeling off or had already fallen on the ground. As we picked one up and examined it more closely, we noticed a random staggered pattern of linear markings we had not seen before. Ultimately the cottage took the form of a long fallen tree with openings following the pattern of markings on the trees. To take another example, Villa The Hague was sparked by our interest in Dutch windmills, their movement and circulation. But in this case, we used the automobile instead of the windmill as an icon of the twentieth century to bring movement to the architecture

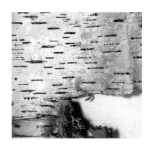

Barry's Bay Cottage

of the villa. The car, incorporated into the structure of the villa, becomes part of the house, providing transportation and acting as an artifact within the house. It is the dynamic spatial momentum
of the villa, however, that captures the spirit of the windmills most vividly.

—

Our inspirations come from many things, as we believe that it is not *what* one looks at but *how* one
looks at the world we live in. Making architecture is not about simply accepting the way things are
but questioning and reinventing the world we want to live in. In rethinking what it is that makes a
home, we hope these projects serve as a testing ground for environments where we can both pro-
tect and transcend the limitations of the body and create an architecture that would be bound
by time and space and yet go beyond time and space.

—

Photograph of Mojgan Hariri (left) and Gisue Hariri (right) by Luca Vignelli

Introduction:
Paul Goldberger

The work of Gisue Hariri and Mojgan Hariri represents modernism at its most optimistic, and at its most realistic. Their designs emerge out of a belief that modernism remains a potent cultural force, but that it has an obligation to respond to the realities of human life and, indeed, that it is likely to realize its highest potential when it acknowledges rather than denies the importance of symbol, of memory, and of sensory experience. For Hariri and Hariri, modern architecture is neither austere nor derivative. The Hariris seek to make buildings that acknowledge the past without replicating it, and that celebrate inventiveness of form without interfering with the processes of daily life. Another way to put this would be to say that the architecture of the Hariris places a high value on both imagination and reality. Theirs is an architecture of balance. It is at once powerful and restrained, self-assured and understated.

—

The Hariris came of age architecturally in the mid-1980s, a time when the reaction against orthodox modernism was at its height, and the failings of what one can now call, without irony, traditional modern architecture seemed manifest. It was not an easy time to enter practice, unless one wanted to design postmodern variations on classical detail, and it is not surprising that the sisters left Cornell, where they had studied under Colin Rowe, and began their careers by going in different directions—Gisue to the unorthodox workshop of Paolo Soleri in Arizona, Mojgan to the more institutional and conventional practice of James Stuart Polshek in New York. Both were forms of escape from an architectural culture that seemed increasingly indifferent to serious exploration of the ongoing possibilities in modernism, although in retrospect these two places, for all they differed, were surely both venues in which the sisters could feel safe from any requirement to spend their days designing pediments and cornices.

—

Their discomfort with the postmodern architecture of the era stemmed, Gisue has said, from their recollections of Iran, where the sisters were born: the architecture they knew from their childhood was what, to them, carried the weight of authenticity, and beside it the American architecture of the 1980s seemed glib, superficial, and facile, particularly in its infatuation with replication. "We had seen the real old architecture in Iran—it was heavy, strong, different. We were uncomfortable with the way of constructing new like old. It wasn't the same," Gisue has said. In 1986, the sisters ended their brief professional separation and reunited to begin their own practice together in New York.

—

Like most young architects, they took what work they got, but they were luckier than most: a handful of clients came their way who shared their view that modernism, far from being exhausted, was ripe for further development, and that there were ways in which to use the modernist vocabulary to produce architecture that would be more sensitive to symbol, to place, and even to history than orthodox modernism had usually been. Their first significant work, a house in New Canaan, Connecticut, of 1990, gave them the chance to design in the midst of the extraordinary array of modern designs from the 1950s that had briefly made New Canaan a vital center of American domestic architecture. The house came at an important time not only in the Hariris' practice, but in the evolution of New Canaan, which was fighting its own battles to support its modernist legacy. The town's early postwar houses were increasingly threatened by buyers who saw only their modest scale and were indifferent to their aesthetic importance, and sought to tear them down to replace them with large Georgian or Tudor mansions. The Hariris' clients, obviously, were different, and the house the sisters designed celebrates the New Canaan legacy and seeks to contribute to its continuation. While it is highly active as a composition—the serenity that marks their work would not be fully developed for a while—it has an ability to be grand without being grandiose that prefigures the gentle assurance of the sisters' later houses. There is something cool and never cold about the Hariris' work; they know how to give a house texture and visual energy, and they have no interest in creating a purely cerebral architecture. It is a compositional architecture, in some ways as dependent on the visual pleasures of composition as the traditional houses that are increasingly its neighbors.

—

In some ways the house that the sisters designed for another client in Greenwich, not far away, a few years later seems even closer to the architectural legacy of New Canaan: it is an understated, and at 3,800 square feet relatively small, house that reads like a set of boxlike forms, with a high central section rising out of a low pavilion, mainly of glass. The reality of the house is somewhat more complex: many of the walls are of translucent fiberglass, which turns the entry hall into a great, two-story lantern, and some of the walls are canted, giving the form an unexpected rhythm and movement.

—

At around the same time, in the mid-1990s, the sisters designed a house for a speculative developer in Great Falls, Virginia, that is in the form of a huge, curving wing, solid and connected to the earth, out of which explodes a high, open wing lifted up on columns and topped by a folded plane roof. It is hard not to think of Frank Lloyd Wright here; although the Hariris are clever enough to make the connections subtle, they have clearly been looking at everything from the Prairie houses to Wright's romantic late work, and the distinct phases of his early and late career seem connected as never before in this house.

—

The relationship of expansive, swooping curves to high, straight masses—which clearly fascinate the Hariris for reasons that go far beyond Wright—was first explored slightly earlier, in a striking waterfront cottage in Ontario, in which a hundred-foot-long wooden structure with a shed roof is set atop a large, curving wood deck. Here the curve exists only in plan, not in section, but it is still a strong presence as it plays off against the straight lines of the cottage. The cottage itself is stark and sumptuous at the same time, somewhere between a lodge and a loft. The unpainted wood exterior and the heavy use of unpainted wood on the inside (along with some corrugated metal) make this building in some ways almost a reinterpretation of an Adirondack camp in modern terms. It is utterly different from the Hariris' urban architecture and yet at the same time it feels a close kinship to it, in much the same way that the Adirondack camps had an odd similarity to the Beaux-Arts mansions that were contemporary to them, and often produced for the same clients.

—

Gisue Hariri has described the design of the Pound Ridge House, of 2002, as being motivated in part by a desire to give great symbolic emphasis to the notion of entry. The front door leads to a large, double-height entry and stair hall, deliberately a bit overscaled for the house. It is surrounded by translucent fiberglass curtain walls, and the sisters are candid in acknowledging their debt to Noguchi—the entry section with its translucent panels is an homage to a Noguchi lamp, elevated to the status of architecture. But the house is more than a simple, neo-Noguchi pavilion. The arrangement of spaces within is rigorous and complex, if spare. The stair wraps around a curved stucco wall, which serves as a counterpoint to the lightness of the translucent facade: once again, curves play off against orthogonal forms. A large hearth dominates the living room—Wright once again, but here, married to a nearly Zen-like serenity in both the facade elevations and the interiors.

—

Surely their finest house, so far, is the Hariris' project for the developer Coco Brown in Sagaponack, New York, completed in 2004. It was the first house to be finished in Brown's ambitious Houses at Sagaponac development, which will eventually include more than two dozen houses by significant architects, mostly of the Hariris' generation. The house has the crisp elegance of classic modernism, but it is sensual and inventive, set to take advantage of its wooded site and designed, like all of the Hariris' work, with a reasonable understanding of the patterns of normal life. There is a private guest wing separated from the rest of the house by a modern version of an open loggia, a huge master suite, and an enormous, open kitchen, all set in an L-shaped structure organized around a pool set into terraces of off-white Turkish travertine. This is minimalism with a certain majesty, not an easy thing at all to pull off.

—

From the pool facade, the view most often photographed, the Sagaponack house seems like an obvious comment on Mies van der Rohe's Barcelona Pavilion. But the Hariris have connected to Mies in the wisest way, not as blind followers but as creative artists, and so the house has a kind of sumptuous, self-assured grandeur that plays on the floating planes and transparent volumes of Mies without ever directly imitating his forms. This is no small accomplishment, to offer a fresh take on an icon. It brings to mind the house Rem Koolhaas produced outside of Paris in the early 1990s, an exceptionally inventive play on Le Corbusier's Villa Savoie, and if the Sagaponack house does not display Koolhaas's wit, neither does it have the dutiful and pious respect that so many Miesians have brought to their work. The Hariris have produced a house that is energetic, strong, serene, and of this moment. It enlivens Mies's notions of architecture even as it reinterprets them with different materials and the different sensibility of a later time. It stands as a reminder not only of how potent Mies's work still is, but of how all of modern architecture, in the right hands, remains so rich in possibility.

—

Sagaponac House

Long Island, New York

2001–2005

This 4,600-square-foot house sits on 2.7 acres of woodland in between the fashionable Southampton and East Hampton areas of Long Island. The structure's spatial configuration invites a variety of personalities and occupants, from hermetic individuals to sociable couples or groups, to be original and invent their own way of habitation.

—

In contrast to most oversized showplaces, suburban mansions, and overstated country houses, this home is composed of two simple rectangular volumes forming an L-shaped plan that engages the landscape and induces a pleasurable sense of being in the country by framing views. The center of the house is the main public space with a swimming pool, multilevel terraces, and a covered porch with a shower. This space is accessible and visible to all other parts of the house, and at times can be seen by neighbors and from the street, becoming a stage for action and display. Similar to the local beaches, the private pool area is a platform for parading bodies to engage in spectatorship and where private fantasies and desires are on exhibit.

—

Inspired by the Swiss artist Alberto Giacometti's sculpture *Figure in a Box between Two Boxes which are Houses*, the Sagaponac House takes the form of a minimalist structure placed on a platform within an untouched natural landscape. A large opening within each rectangular volume frames the private life in the house and the pool beyond. These openings investigate the cultural definition of the domestic enclosure, revealing private and public hidden motivations, social interactions, and exchange within and beyond the house.

—

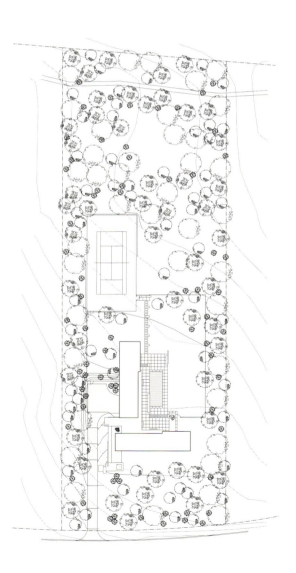

Site Plan

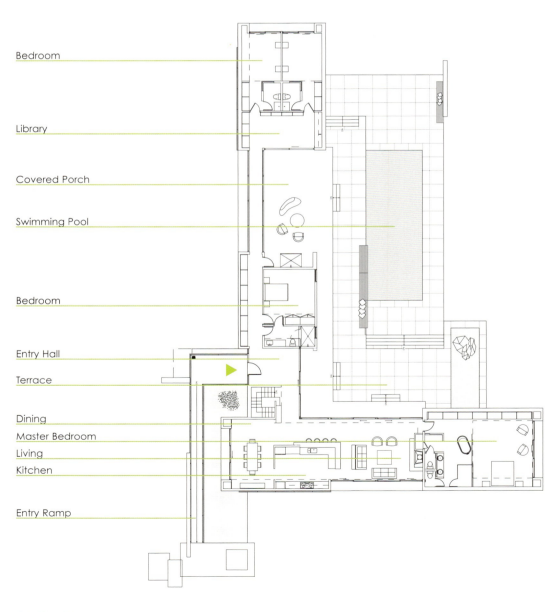

Bedroom

Library

Covered Porch

Swimming Pool

Bedroom

Entry Hall

Terrace

Dining
Master Bedroom
Living
Kitchen

Entry Ramp

First-Floor Plan

Aqua House

Miami Beach, Florida

2000–2005

This three-story, 4,500-square-foot town house was designed as part of a new development called AQUA on Allison Island, in Miami Beach. This enclave is designed as a planned neighborhood that would offer an alternative to a row of high-rise condominiums known as Condo Canyon in this very desirable resort town. Planned by the urban design firm of Andres Duany and Elizabeth Plater-Zyberk, AQUA will feature a combination of mid-rise apartment buildings and rows of town houses built in a pedestrian-friendly environment where the water's edge is shared by everyone. Here, a combination of traditional urban and modern architecture embodies an original vision.

—

The Aqua House was inspired by the movement of watercrafts and vessels around Allison Island and the Miami Beach waterways. The main body of the house takes the form of a sculpture carved out of a solid block. The curved metal roofs arching in different directions allow the top to appear fluid, dynamically reflecting the sunlight.

—

The design reinterprets the streamlined art deco architecture of Miami, breaking down the hegemony of cubic forms, and offers a powerful combination of curves and horizontality in a completely new architecture for Miami.

—

Traditionally, town houses are entered from the narrow width of the lot; this house being at the end of the block raised the challenge of articulating three facades while entering the house from the long side. Contrary to most traditional plans where public spaces such as the living, dining, and kitchen areas are located on the ground floor, those of the Aqua House hover above ground, occupying the second floor and the rooftop, and allowing for uninterrupted views of the waterways and sunsets.

—

Entering the house through a courtyard, a spacious foyer leads to three bedrooms on the first floor on one end and a staircase on the other. The sculptural stair to the second floor arrives at a large open loft containing the living, dining, kitchen, and family rooms and a spacious terrace offering spectacular views. The third floor is the most private and is dedicated to the master suite. The roof garden accommodates the studio/entertainment room and is distinguished by a wraparound viewing deck.

—

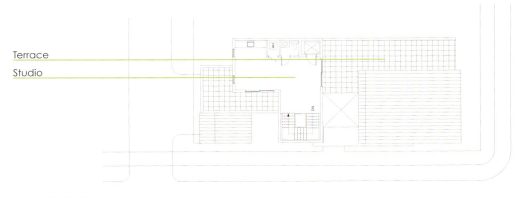

Terrace
Studio

Tower/Studio Plan

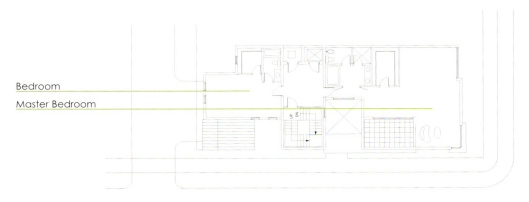

Bedroom
Master Bedroom

Third-Floor Plan

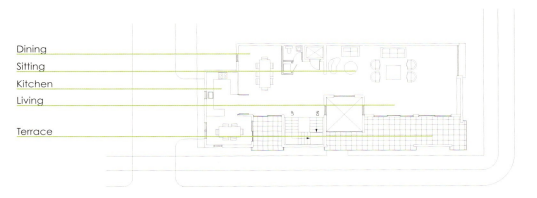

Dining
Sitting
Kitchen
Living
Terrace

Second-Floor Plan

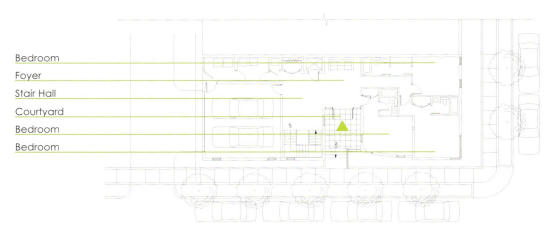

Bedroom
Foyer
Stair Hall
Courtyard
Bedroom
Bedroom

First-Floor Plan

Park Avenue Loft

New York City

2003–2004

Located in a postwar tower in the Carnegie Hill area of New York City, this project combines two apartments into one large dwelling composed of three bedrooms, three and a half bathrooms, a study/guest room, and an open living, dining, and kitchen area. The plan is organized in an L shape with a core of wet areas in the center. All public spaces form a rectangular volume along Park Avenue within an open plan, challenging the traditional layout of most apartments on the Upper East Side. A row of large, horizontal windows along the exterior wall creates a continuity via a long, floating cabinet allowing the interior space to extend into the space of Park Avenue. Living and dining spaces, however, are defined by two sculptural "folding planes." These elements not only separate and connect different areas, but also allow for hardwiring of the loft without lowering the entire ceiling area to accommodate the lighting fixtures. Adjacent to the dining area is the kitchen/family room. A large metal and glass sliding panel conceals and reveals the kitchen from the living/dining area. Perpendicular to the public loft space are the private quarters, where the bedrooms are organized in a row along a small hallway. The master suite is spare and quiet with a Zen platform bed and a sitting/reading room that acts as a Hall of Fame for selected children's art-work. A large master bathroom in stone accommodates two separate but connected his-and-her areas, each with a sink, toilet, and a bathtub with shower, a luxury often missing in many classic Park Avenue apartments.

Kitchen/Family Room

Dining

Living

Bedroom

Bedroom

Master Suite

Floor Plan

Belmont House

Belmont, California

1999–2002

Unlike the mega McMansions of recent years that dot California and specifically the San Francisco Bay area, this 3,000-square-foot house built into a hill in the city of Belmont is an efficient, direct, and simple home. The owners are a young couple with a small child who work in Silicon Valley and are part of the digital culture generation of the region.

—

Unlike superficial historical reproductions, this project explores the fusion between two popular vernacular architectures of the region: the mobile trailer home and the Mexican pueblo, creating a vertical hybrid of two different cultures and inspiring a new generation living in the area.

—

The design begins with a curved concrete retaining wall, which provides an edge for the driveway and leads uphill. A series of concrete steps extend from the driveway to the mid-entry level. A long, modern veranda with a blue stucco wall guides visitors to an oversized, rusted steel door. This dramatic portal pivots into the entrance hall where a staircase then rises to the upper main floor.

—

Inspired by Mexican pueblo architecture, the lower level of the house is composed of heavy, textured, colorful walls. This level includes the entrance/art gallery on the east side and the children's quarter on the west. A staircase joins the entranceway to the upper main level, where the master suite occupies one end and loft space including the dining, kitchen, and library spaces and a home office at the other end all open onto a terrace with views of the hillside in the back.

—

Inspired by the industrial generation of mobile homes, the upper level is a rectangular volume wrapped in metal, floating over its solid base; it is light and hovers over the first floor as if ready to move on. This volume is distinguished by large openings on both the hill and valley sides, allowing for a cross breeze and a visual panorama of the hillside. Expressed here is the paradoxical human desire to partake of the new and the old, the heavy and the light, the earth and the sky, the rooted and the mobile simultaneously.

—

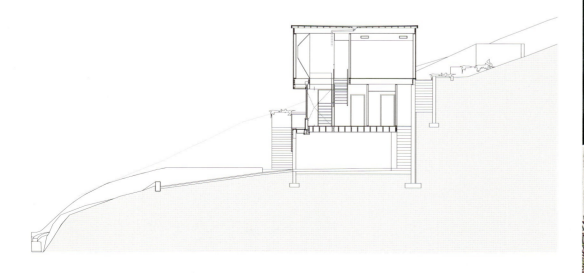

Section

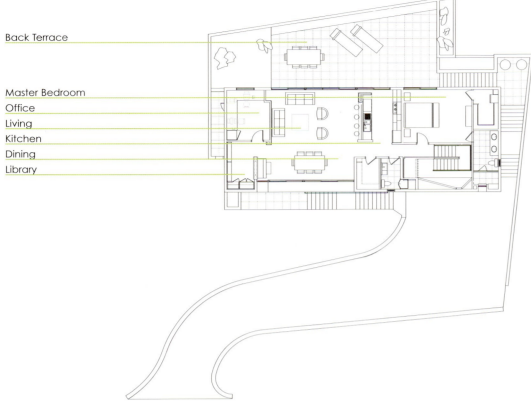

Back Terrace

Master Bedroom
Office
Living
Kitchen
Dining
Library

Second-Floor Plan

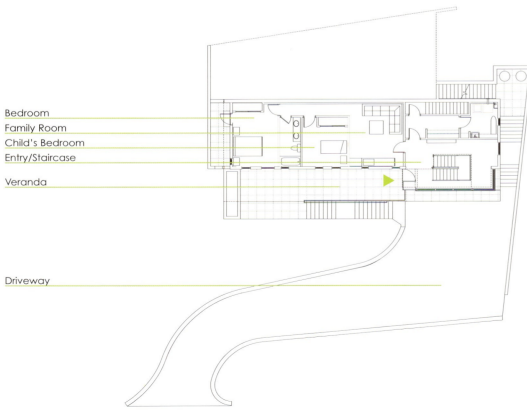

Bedroom
Family Room
Child's Bedroom
Entry/Staircase

Veranda

Driveway

First-Floor Plan

Perry Street Loft

New York City

2000–2002

Inspired by Isamu Noguchi's stone sculptures and translucent Akari lamps, this 4,500-square-foot home was designed on the highest elevation of a 5-acre property in a calm, tranquil, and quiet, Zen-like setting. Surrounded by tall trees and rock outcropping, the architecture of this home interprets and internalizes this landscape, offering the intangible properties of time and light. The house is conceptually a simplified and abstract "garden" in stone, wood, metal, and translucent walls, whose architecture is composed of three interlocking volumes: the entry, living, and fitness/meditation volumes.

—

The entry volume is a vertical space, two-and-a-half stories high and takes the shape of a vertical void forming the hearth of the house. This void contains different levels and provides the vertical and horizontal circulation to other parts of the house. It is enclosed by translucent, fiberglass curtain walls, which allow soft light into the space while a series of clear glass windows frame the landscape. The main element of this volume is a staircase that wraps around a curved stucco wall and connects different parts and levels of the house. This highly sculpted and articulated space becomes the internal landscape emphasizing the void of our existence in this passing world and emitting light at night just like a Noguchi Akari lamp.

—

The living volume contains the private quarters (bedrooms) on the lower floor with the public spaces (living/dining) up above. The fitness/meditation volume joins the living and entry volume via the kitchen/family room on one level and the gym on the lower level with the garage.

—

This house captures the very essence of nature through tactility of material, light, and space and provokes dynamic reactions and emotions from its occupants.

—

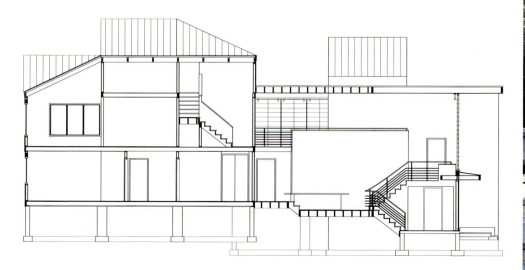

Section

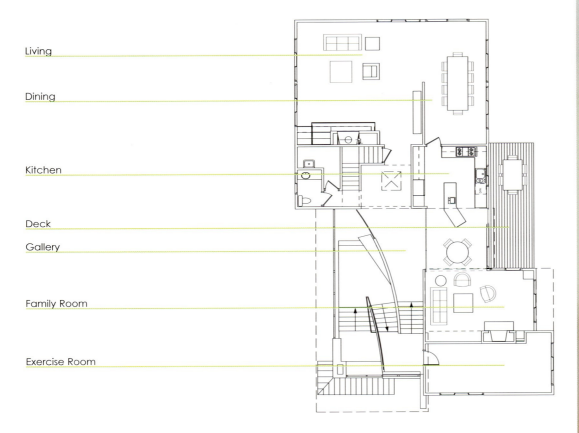

Living

Dining

Kitchen

Deck

Gallery

Family Room

Exercise Room

Second-Floor Plan

Master Bedroom

Bedroom

Master Bath

Bedroom

Office

Entry Hall

Garage

Entry Vestibule

First-Floor Plan

The Digital House

The Un-Private House Exhibition, MoMA, New York City

1999–2000

This project explores the nature of domestic space in the new millennium by examining the changing habits of the family structure, the institution of marriage, children, older adults, and single sex families; communication and information technologies, work, leisure, the public and private; and conception of the body, health, and hygiene.

—

The physical form of a typical home is in flux. Changes in the institution of marriage and family structure require programmatic and spatial updating as more and more individuals find they are working, shopping, teaching, entertaining, and working out at home.

—

This house's design is based on the fact that most daily activities can now take place at home as a result of new digital technology and global telecommunication and networking. The house is organized around a touch-activated digital spine liquid with a global network database. The spine is a steel structure enclosed in glass made of active matrix liquid crystal displays (AMLCDs).

—

The architecture of the structure's main spaces has been reduced to simple, efficient, and minimal habitable units, partially prefabricated and available off the shelf. These areas plug into the steel structure of the spine similar to an industrial shelving unit.

—

The Digital House is for a family of three independent beings free from preconceived notions of gender roles, domination, and sexual orientation. The architecture of this house allows its occupants to interact virtually yet live together actually, addressing the paradoxical American desire for a solitary existence while at the same time accommodating notions of community.

—

This house presents the opportunity to meditate on the following poetic concepts, as outlined by John Brehm in the text accompanying the presentation of the project as part of the Museum of Modern Art's "Un-Private House" exhibition:

_ If the house is an extension of the body or a transparency of the mind, what will the house of the next millennium look like? A house that both protects and transcends the limitations of the body. A house that is bound by time and space and yet beyond time and space. A house that reflects the changing configurations of family, work, play, communication, and virtual and actual realities.

_ A Digital House.

_ In this house, the central walls are made from Liquid Crystal Displays, the building blocks of the future. These walls are capable not merely of separating and enclosing space within the house but of collapsing the very idea of time and space. Here meals can be prepared with the help of a virtual chef from a favorite restaurant and one can have dinner with friends who live thousands of miles away.

_ The corridors of the digital house are no longer "empty spaces," or a "waste of time," but an opportunity for heightened awareness.

_ In the digital house, the comfort, safety, and stability of home can coexist with the risky possibilities of flight.

_ In the twenty-first century, as more and more jobs are performed from home, the temporal and spatial constraints of work become less rigid, as the keyboard rather than the car or commuter train takes us where we need to go.

_ Connecting the main areas are the transient spaces, which allow the inhabitants to unplug themselves momentarily (going up the spiral stair) as they move between tasks and from the virtual to the actual world. Here the eye takes in a layering of realities as one can look into other parts of the house, to the landscape beyond the house, or to the images on the walls.

_ The house of the next millennium is more than a home, it is an embodiment of our dreams. Each bedroom is therefore equipped with a Dream-Recording Device, so that the flight of the dreaming mind can be traced, its images replayed and studied for evidence of who we are or what the future has in store for us.

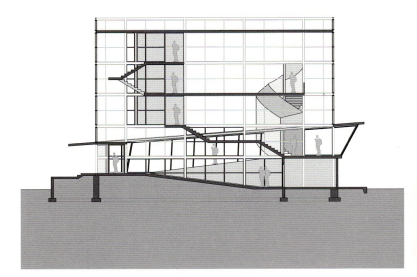

Longitudinal Section

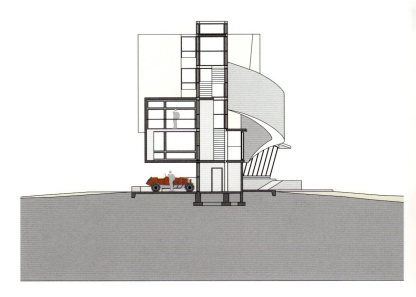

Transverse Section

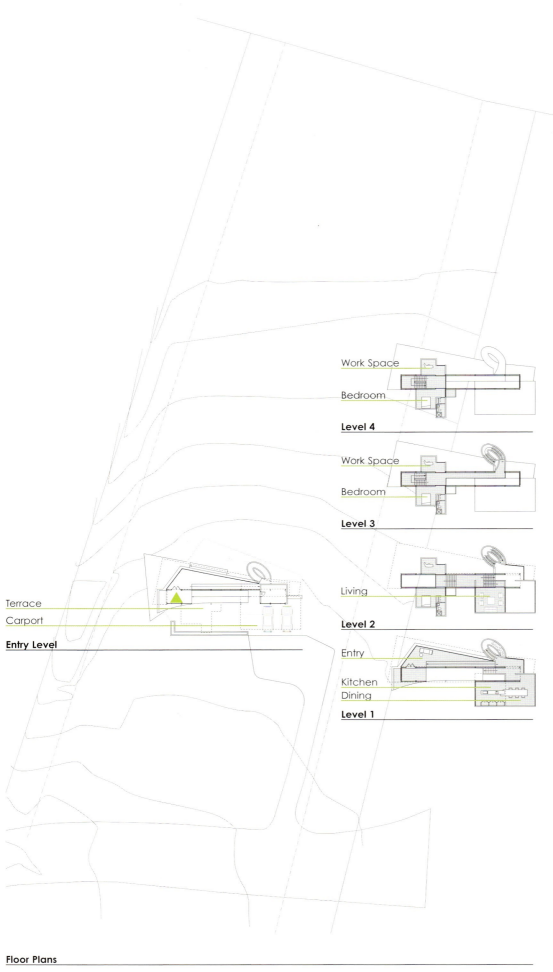

Work Space

Bedroom

Level 4

Work Space

Bedroom

Level 3

Living

Level 2

Terrace

Carport

Entry Level

Entry

Kitchen

Dining

Level 1

Floor Plans

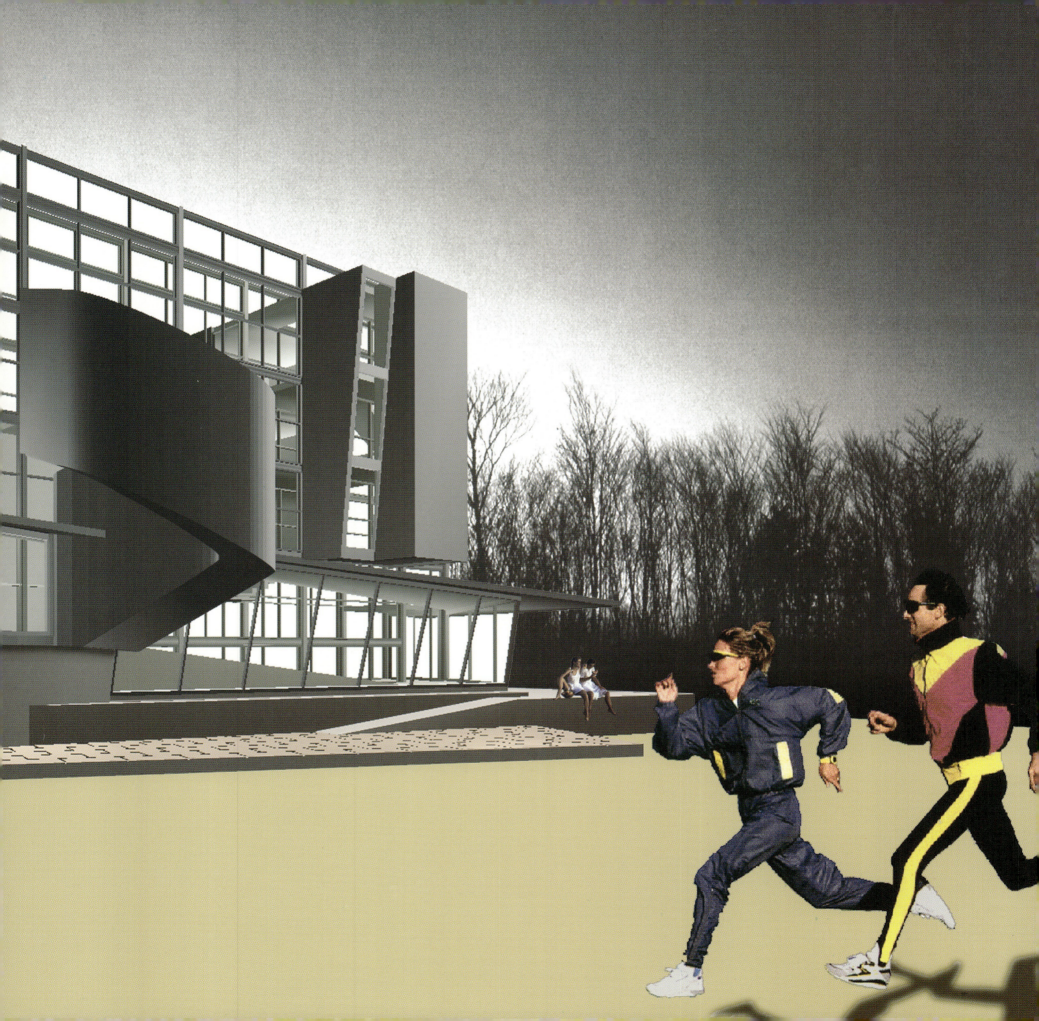

PUMPKIN PIE

1 CUP CANNED PUMPKIN
  PUREE
1/4 CUP GRANULATED
  SUGAR
1/2 TEASPOON CINNAMON
1/2 TEASPOON GINGER
1/4 TEASPOON FRESHLY
  GRATED NUTMEG
1/4 TEASPOON GROUND
  ALLSPICE

1/4 TEASPOON COCOA
  POWDER
1/4 TEASPOON SALT
  LARGE EGGS
  HEAVY CREAM
  BLESPOON
  OLASSES
  ASPOON PURE
  ILLA EXTRACT

ACCEPTED BY SERVER

A1
A2
A3
S1
S2

Fifth Avenue Penthouse

New York City

1997–1998

This penthouse located in one of New York City's landmark buildings has a wraparound terrace with views of the Washington Square Arch, the Hudson River, and the majestic Empire State Building. Inspired by its site and iconic views, the main floor of the apartment is essentially an open area with a continuous limestone floor, inviting the city elements to become part of this new landscape. All existing walls and fixtures were removed and the beams and columns of the original structure were exposed and brought forth. Treating the structure like an archaeological site, a few water and waste pipes were found in the center of the space. Celebrating these elements by having them cleaned and displayed in a showcase of metal and glass, they became a central architectural component of the space.

—

The design of the apartment is organized around a simple composition of planes and volumes. A pearwood cabinet in the living room accommodates the stereo system while a cantilevered plane in the dining area is used as a serving counter. The ceiling is a sculpted plane containing the central air-conditioning ducts and structural beams. A staircase connects the living area to the above private, bedroom/library suite, a two-part arrangement of planes and volumes which begins with a volumetric composition in stone and then transforms into a series of cantilevered cherrywood planes supported by stainless steel folded brackets.

—

The client's desire for a quiet, contemplative, and monastic environment and his love for books are reflected throughout the apartment but especially in the library, where book cases of maplewood pivot to open and close the room. These pivoting planes also reveal and conceal the client's collection of rare and valuable books.

—

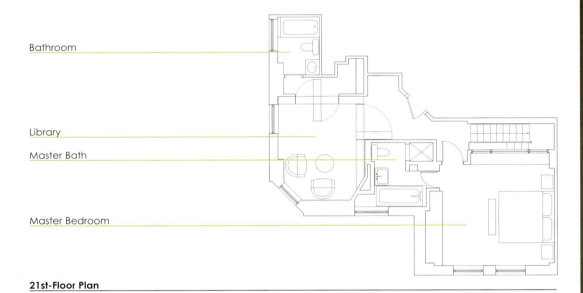

Bathroom

Library

Master Bath

Master Bedroom

21st-Floor Plan

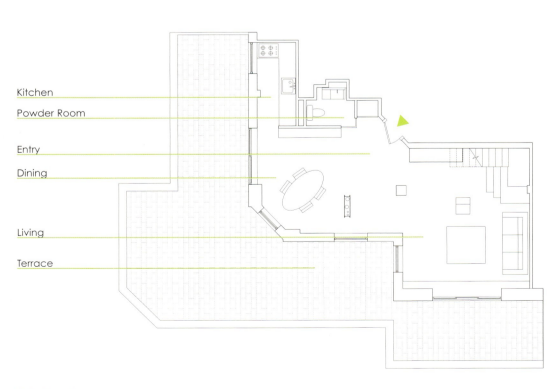

Kitchen

Powder Room

Entry

Dining

Living

Terrace

20th-Floor Plan

Greenwich House

Greenwich, Connecticut

1996–
1998

This 3,800-square-foot suburban home commissioned by a young Argentinian couple with three children presented an opportunity to investigate and reexamine the potential possibilities of a suburban home in the new millennium. The owner's paradoxical love/hate relationship with both urban and suburban life led to an evaluation of the changing attitudes of a new generation of homeowners toward privacy and space versus public interaction and urban density.

—

Conceptually, a new datum line or ground plane was established by partially using an existing rectangular structure to create a new, one-story, horizontal, L-shaped volume, containing the children's bedrooms and the gym in the east wing and the living, dining, kitchen, eat-in area, laundry, maid's suite, and garages in the west wing. The two wings in the center of the house are connected by an open media room with a large-screen television and state-of-the-art digital telecommunication equipment, linking the inhabitants globally to the rest of the world.

—

Inspired by rock formations punctuating the surrounding landscape, a cluster of vertical volumes, each in a different geometrical form, penetrates the center of the house creating a dramatic urban entrance. The main walls of the house on the north and south are enclosed by translucent fiberglass curtain walls occasionally interrupted by sections of clear glass that give a glimpse of life inside the private quarters.

—

A virtual and actual transparency beginning in the entrance hall continues up to the master bedroom suite, the highest room in the house. Under the angled roof of the bedroom suite a frame of industrial windows inserted within the grid of the translucent wall resembling a shoji screen offers views of the surrounding landscape. This room is a place of solitude and dreams where it is possible to contemplate the interplay between being and non-being. Filled with an abundance of calm, soft, filtered light during the day, this house is transformed into a lighthouse at night, emitting and radiating its inner glow and being.

—

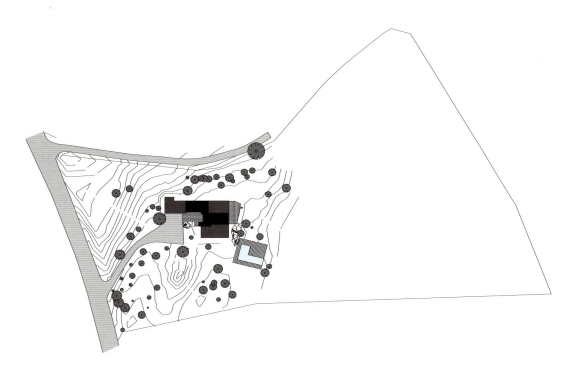

Site Plan

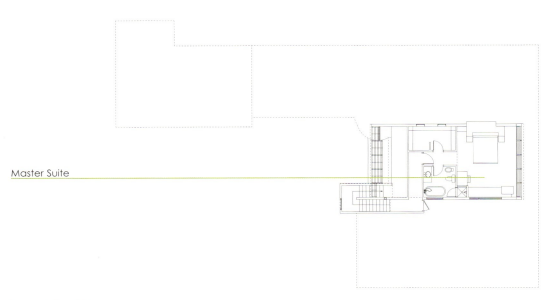

Master Suite

Second-Floor Plan

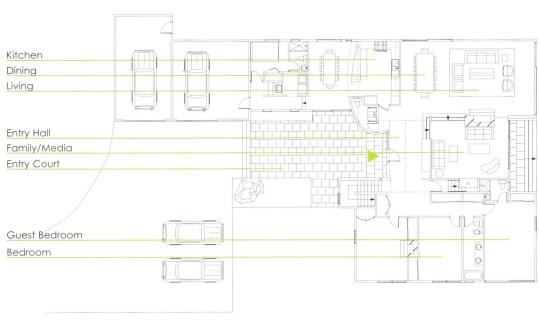

Kitchen
Dining
Living

Entry Hall
Family/Media
Entry Court

Guest Bedroom
Bedroom

First-Floor Plan

Riverbend House

Great Falls, Virginia

1994–1997

This 5,000-square-foot house was built on speculation by a developer in Great Falls, Virginia, serving as a testing ground for a new generation of speculative home buyers.

—

The design scheme of this project challenges standard expectations of suburban homes, including concepts of resale value, superficiality of appearance, and the American dream. Contrary to the traditionally styled house's opulent facade, with enormous porticoes (supported by vinyl Corinthian columns), the entry to this home provides the experience of arrival in the space of the in-between. The entrance slips between two walls, creating a well-marked but simple introduction to the interior.

—

The site is a heavily wooded landscape, sloping sharply down to a creek through which water, bending and moving, becomes a major element, creating a contemplative sound, a reminder of the passage of time within the stillness of the setting. The house is divided into two parts, spatially, formally, programatically, and structurally. One part is earthbound, characterized by a heavy masonry structure that follows the contour and curvature of the land. This curved volume creates an entry court and contains the private quarters (bedrooms, kitchen, and guest suite). The second part is sky bound, with a light, winglike structure that floats above the earth, supported by steel columns; it is mostly enclosed by glass walls. This section accommodates the public areas (family, dining, and living rooms) and is roofed with a precisely formed folded plane; lifting upward as it stretches over the house, it emphasizes the human desire for weightlessness.

—

At its base, the house spreads out onto a large, open terrace that is well integrated into the structure and the existing landscape, and replaces the typical "front and back lawn" of suburban living.

—

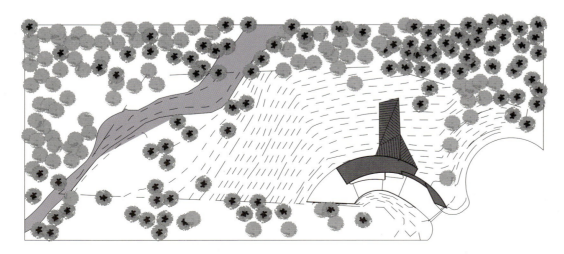

Site Plan

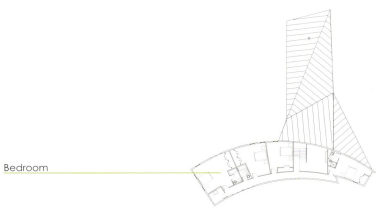

Bedroom

Second-Floor Plan

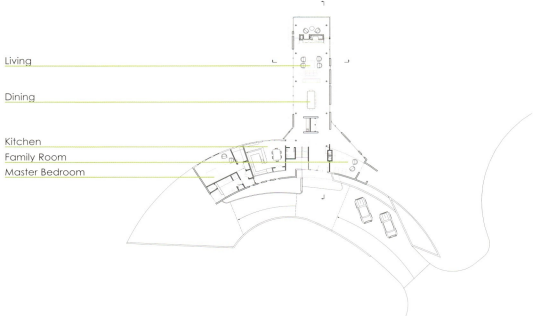

Living

Dining

Kitchen
Family Room
Master Bedroom

First-Floor Plan

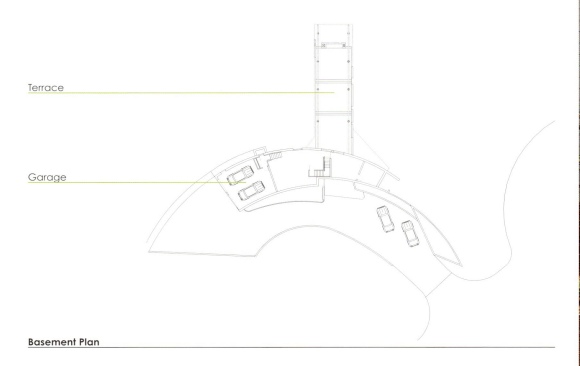

Terrace

Garage

Basement Plan

Spartan House

The Hague, Netherlands

1993–1997

Built as part of a housing project in the Hague, Netherlands, the urban planning of this narrow strip of land was designed by the Office for Metropolitan Architecture and consisted of eight lots in two rows, each lot measuring 33 x 39 feet with a small footprint (26 x 33 feet) for a single-family home. The developer selected eight architects and assigned each to a lot with a common set of criteria and zoning restrictions. The participating architects assigned to the front row, facing a typical Dutch canal, were Bernard Tschumi, Marc Mack, Steven Holl, and Andrew MacNair. The architects assigned to the back row, facing a boulevard, were Henry Ciriani, Frank Israel, Hariri & Hariri, and Stefano De Martino.

—

For this Spartan House, the given envelope was cut into two volumes, conceptually creating a path from the street to the canal. One volume accommodates the vertical circulation (staircase) and service areas (storage, laundry) and is wrapped in a corrugated galvanized steel, creating a spartan edge on the west side of the house. The second volume is a narrow brick box typical of most Dutch homes. It is a simple, utilitatrian volume containing an open loft space for living, dining, and kitchen areas on the first floor with a row of bedrooms on the upper level. This impenetrable private domain has porthole openings on the east side, connecting this living vessel poetically to the canal while providing circular lenses to allow light into the rooms.

—

The most dynamic area is the space where the cut takes place, a double-story space stretching from the entry to the other end of the house that not only becomes a connector between different parts of the structure, but a path between two sections of the site: the boulevard Dedemsvaartweg and the canal.

—

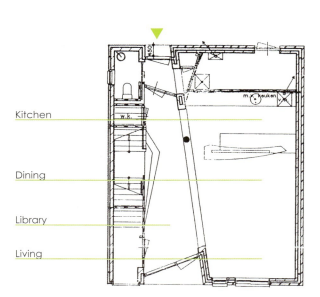

Kitchen

Dining

Library

Living

First-Floor Plan

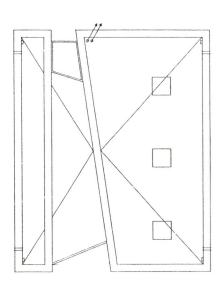

Roof Plan

Barry's Bay Cottage

Ontario, Canada

1991– 1994

This 2,500-square-foot cottage houses a family of six that had outgrown the old, prefabricated A-frame cottage existing on the site, a rural parcel of land in Ontario, Canada, sloping gently down to the freshwater Lake Kamaniskeg and surrounded by evergreens and tall birch trees.

—

The client's sentimental attachment to the old cottage resulted in keeping the original structure as a children's guest house, shoring up its leaning and faulty foundation, consequently treating the existing cottage as a given.

—

The new cottage is a 100-foot-long wood structure stretching along the western property line, only three feet away from the existing structure. This tight condition preserves trees and open space in front of the existing cottage while creating a peculiar tension between the old and the new, a common occurrence in farm structures.

—

The existing and the new creations are connected by a large wood deck. Lifted above grade on concrete piers, changing form as one proceeds toward the lake, this runwaylike deck compresses one between the two buildings, at first revealing a narrow, framed view of the lake. Further procession finds the view opening gradually as one approaches the end of the deck, some ten feet above the earth. A small structure designed for outdoor showers completes this complex at the end of the deck. The shower provides an intimate space, with framed views of the lake, to reflect while cleansing oneself from preconceived notions of everyday life.

—

The slot windows on the east side of the new house were inspired by horizontal markings on the bark of the surrounding birch trees. These slot openings funnel outside light into narrow beams inside. At night they act as exterior light fixtures and during the day they frame different parts of the landscape beyond. In contrast, the west side emphasizes the verticality of the adjacent field of tall trees through a vertical span of windows and a stair tower wrapped in corrugated metal.

—

The interior of the new cottage includes a large living space with a freestanding fireplace at its center. On the upper level an open bridge connects the reading room to the library, all open to the living room below and the master suite at the north end. A shaded upper deck adjacent to the reading room allows privacy for contemplation and rest.

—

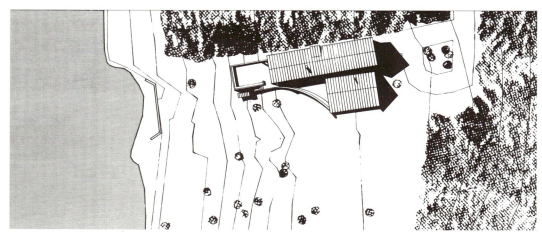

Site Plan

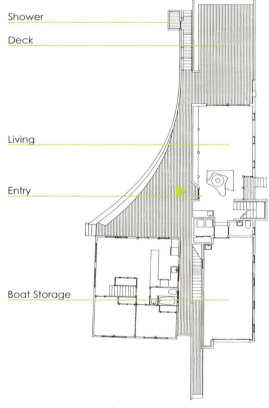

Shower

Deck

Living

Entry

Boat Storage

First-Floor Plan

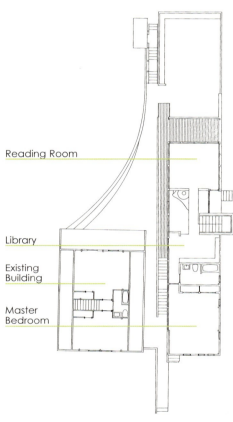

Reading Room

Library

Existing
Building

Master
Bedroom

Second-Floor Plan

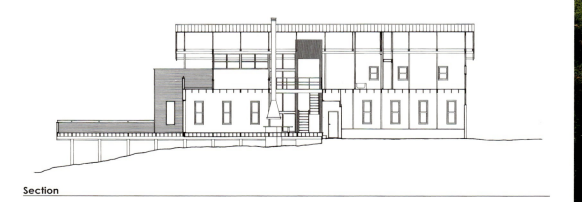

Section

170

Villa The Hague

The Hague, Netherlands

1991–1992

This project, or "urban villa," for a single family in the Hague, Netherlands, is one of a series of eight villas being developed as part of a housing exhibition. The project's significance is its possibility to lend itself as a prototype for speculative housing development in the post–cold war era; enforcing a set of strict urban guidelines, while allowing for individual architectural expression.

—

The site is a small plot (49 x 52 feet, buildable area of 33 x 39 feet) with a given program of four bedrooms, three bathrooms, a living room, kitchen, dining room, and carport. The villa assumes two completely different attitudes toward the site. The facade facing the boulevard is a planar expanse of wall, reinforcing the bound edge of the site's envelope, while those facing the common alley on the canal side are more expansive of the spaces they accommodate. Typical of many Dutch urban row houses, the first floor is more open and transparent, allowing light as well as the glance of the occasional passerby or motorist to penetrate the structure. It is this idea of openness, extracted from the vernacular, which became one of the constructs investigated in the design of this project.

—

The street facade is perhaps the first indication of the overlapping nature of the villa. Within the frame created by the wall is the curvilinear stair as it arches over the owner's automobile, but it is actually possible to see down into the living space and into the yard beyond. The car, now encapsulated and incorporated by the structure of the villa, becomes part of the house.

—

The villa becomes a Gestaltist puzzle in which the overlapping of the spaces becomes a contiguous part of a greater architectural whole. Behind the orthogonally oriented street facade, the building begins to splay away from its origins, revealing a spatial momentum that continues throughout the house and upward to the clad metal roofs. The structure of the villa, concrete columns and flat slabs supporting a cavity-brick masonry wall, allows the upper kinetic volumes to float over the more transparent first floor. The kinetic form of the house on the canal side responds to the flow and movement of boats passing by.

—

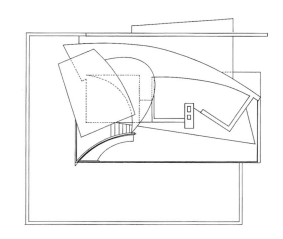

Roof Plan

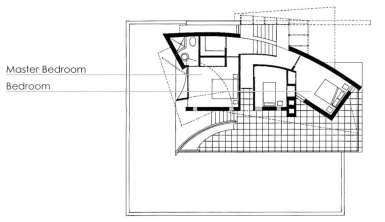

Master Bedroom
Bedroom

Third-Floor Plan

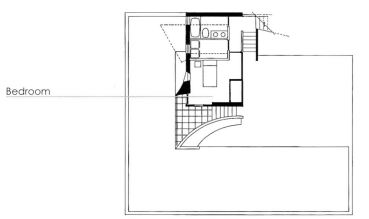

Bedroom

Second-Floor Plan

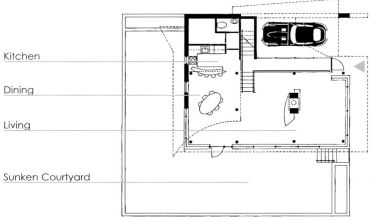

Kitchen

Dining

Living

Sunken Courtyard

First-Floor Plan

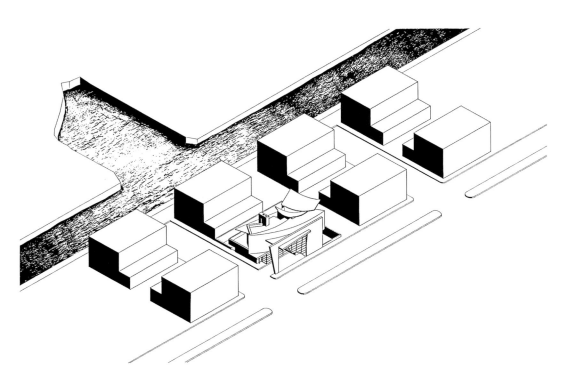

Axonometric View

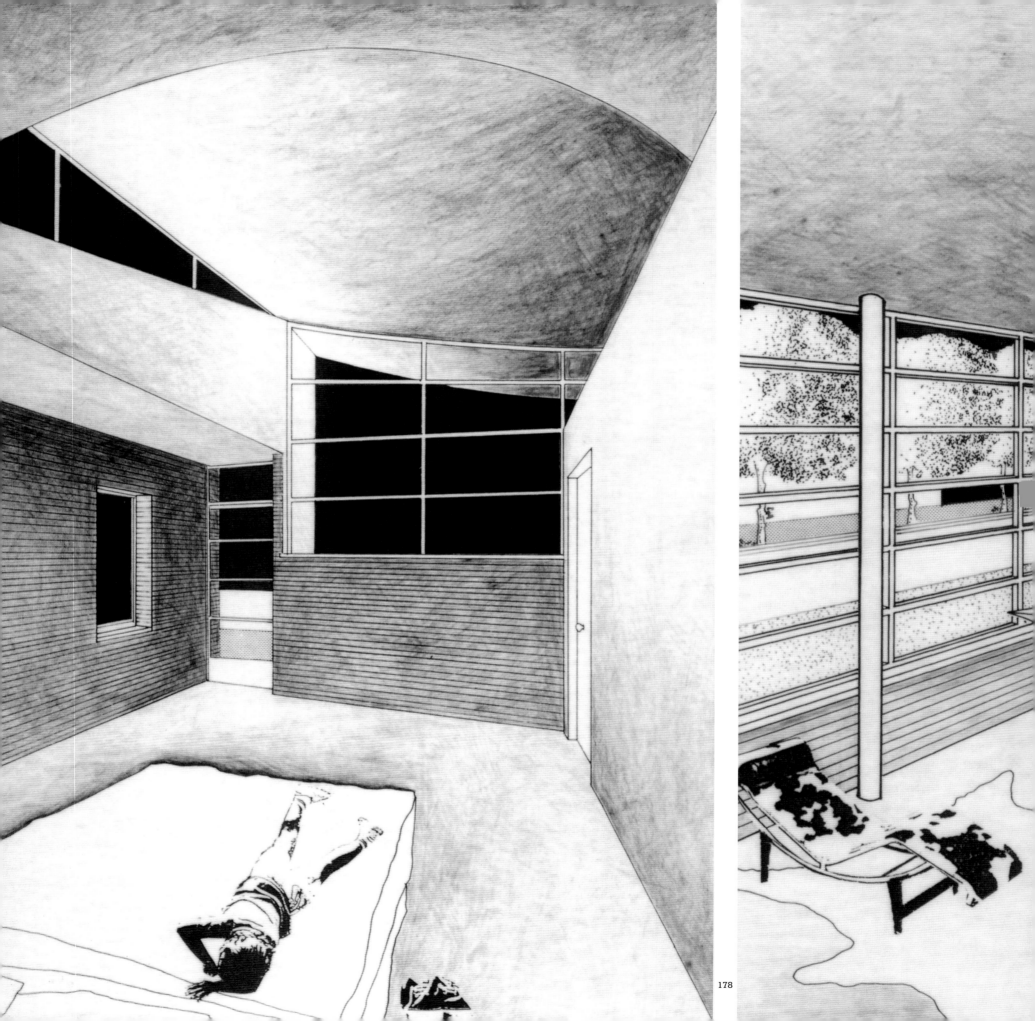

New Canaan House

New Canaan, Connecticut

1989–1991

The town of New Canaan, Connecticut, has a history of modern architecture that has inspired many contemporary architects. In the years following World War II, an unusual number of talented architects interested in the International Style and experimentation gathered here—including Philip Johnson, Frank Lloyd Wright, and Marcel Breuer—contributing not only to the history of the town but also to the history of architecture.

This project is an addition to and a renovation of a carriage house built around 1900. A study, dining room, and kitchen were added in 1950, and a two-car garage in 1956. The site is a rural two-and-a-half-acre parcel, sparsely wooded with a row of trees separating it from the adjacent property. The vernacular architecture of the area is known for its barns, covered bridges, and carriage houses. These vernacular features were analyzed, reinterpreted, and used as the main elements of the house, while the siting and interpenetration of the elements followed the modern cubist ideology of space-making.

One of the program's requisites was the creation of a uniform identity for the new and old structures. A common entryway was created to tie the old and new structures together. The intention was to create an interplay of volumes within the familiar forms native to the rural northeast.

These volumes were conceived initially as independent structures which, through the exercise of volumetric penetration, began to connect and fit together precisely. The fact that the house's volumes were structurally framed independently of each other allows each volumetric piece to retain its identity while becoming part of the greater architectural whole. From this system of operation, a number of distinctly different and autonomous spaces come together to create a harmonious architectural work.

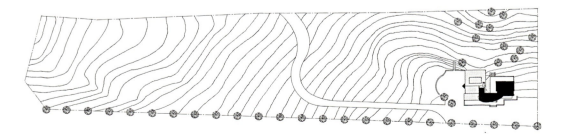

Site Plan

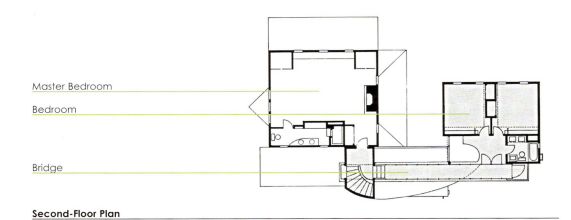

Master Bedroom

Bedroom

Bridge

Second-Floor Plan

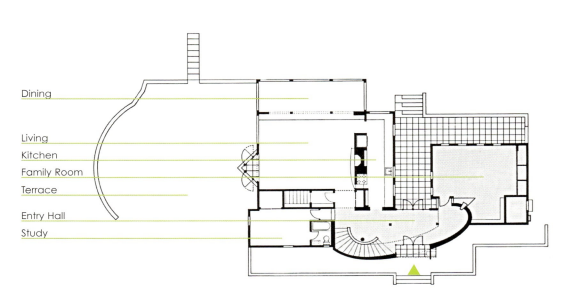

Dining

Living

Kitchen

Family Room

Terrace

Entry Hall

Study

First-Floor Plan

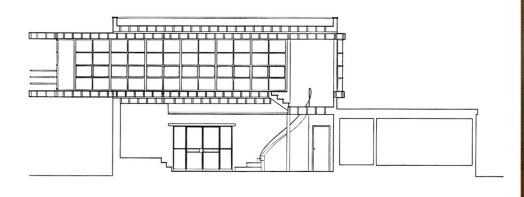

Section

Soho Loft

New York City

1986–1988

This project is a renovation of a duplex loft in Soho, an "artist's loft" with the high ceilings and open space typical of the late-nineteenth-century cast-iron buildings of this former industrial district. The intention was to retain the characteristics of the existing loft while transforming it into a habitable space for the client. The lower level was kept relatively open, and the required spaces were organized around two parallel walls, the fireplace wall and the dividing wall between the study and living area. The fireplace wall is treated with rough, hand-trawled stucco, with a punched-in log box and a linear marble mantel. The dividing wall is a freestanding plaster wall, emphasized by two oversized steel-and-glass doors for the full-size openings on either side.

Replacing the existing spiral staircase to resolve the vertical circulation between the two levels presented a challenging situation. Due to the number of rotations and the treads' open grating, the staircase vibrated beyond normal expectations, making ascending and descending frightening experiences. However, the five-foot-by-five-foot opening in the ceiling could not be enlarged. After many attempts, a hybrid stair, partially straight and partially spiral, was developed. The two stairs are structurally independent but are unified by a single sheet of steel curving in a logarithmic spiral. The experience of moving on this stair is like being on a Möbius strip—one is simultaneously inside and outside the steel sheet. The stair railings terminate in a circular pattern of rings, which is also used in the design of the pendant light fixture and bar stools.

The client's passion for the color blue is accommodated throughout the loft in a variety of shades: the wood floors are light blue-gray; the library walls are deep Florentine blue; the doors are steel blue; the bar countertop is in blue marble. On the upper level, where the master suite and roof garden are located, the blue tint is softer. The roof garden is composed of a rose arbor and a wisteria trellis, all made of cedar, and a spiral staircase completing the journey upward to the private sun deck.

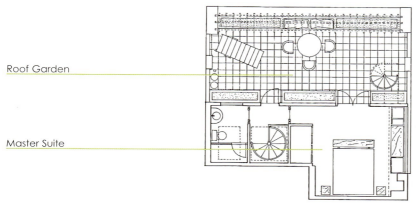

Roof Garden

Master Suite

Upper-Level Plan

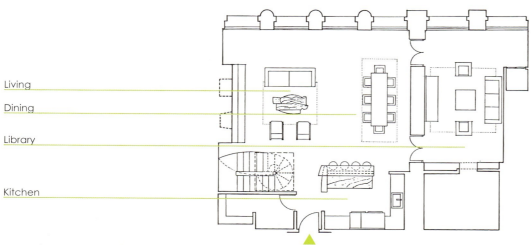

Living

Dining

Library

Kitchen

Lower-Level Plan

Essay:
John Brehm

Stillness at the Center: The Architecture of Hariri and Hariri

But if a house is a living value, it must integrate an element of unreality . . .
—GASTON BACHELARD, *THE POETICS OF SPACE*

Before looking at the Hariris' extraordinary architecture and interior spaces, I must begin with a disclaimer: I am not an architect or an architectural critic. My knowledge of architecture is entirely of an intuitive nature, which either disqualifies me from saying anything useful on the subject or affords me the wisdom of beginner's mind. I am a poet and have known Mojgan Hariri and Gisue Hariri since we were at Cornell together in the early 1980s. I remember that they often remarked on the fresco of poet and architect holding hands that adorned Cornell's Sage Chapel. Certainly, in the Hariris' work, poetry and architecture join hands, and the results are poetic in the best and deepest sense of the word.

—

I would like to enter the Hariris' houses by way of another word, and that word is "room." Like the words "home" and "womb," in "room" we find the om sound which mystics for centuries have heard as a cosmic vibration, the basic frequency humming beneath all our human noise; a sound that reminds us of the vastness and emptiness and stillness of primordial space. Are such word echoes accidental? Is there a deeper relationship between *room* and *womb* and *om*? How beautiful it would be to find the ancient speaker who first voiced the sound *room* (*rūm* in Old English) and ask her why she chose it, or why it came to her, and why others accepted and repeated it. We are left to imagine such an interview, but for me the sound of the word "room" conjures both openness and enclosure, clarity and warmth, stillness and freedom—a fertile source from which the mind may give birth to imagination and imagination to spirit.

—

In the Hariris' rooms, with their openness, their spaciousness, their air of calm repose, one feels an underlying spiritual aesthetic—a kind of spiritual minimalism—shaping and informing their designs. These rooms seem to present an externalization of inner clarity and to demand a state of mindfulness from their inhabitants. The floating stairway in the Hariris' Fifth Avenue Penthouse, with its steps that cantilever out from the wall into empty space, is as airy as a staircase can be. I have walked up those stairs and felt, more vividly than ever before or since, the physicality, the precariousness, of rising from one floor to another. One is aware of one's feet upon each step, as in a walking meditation, and the experience fulfills Gaston Bachelard's insistence that a house must integrate an element of unreality if it is to have a living value.

—

Stairs and staircases are in fact among the Hariris' most distinctive achievements. It's clear that for these architects, rising or descending a stair, or moving between rooms, is not simply a momentary and meaningless gap between one experience and another, but an opportunity for heightened awareness of what one is leaving and where one is arriving. Their signature twisted steel staircase in the Soho Loft, with its sculptural strength that spirals up like a splice of DNA and from which it is hard to remove one's gaze, epitomizes this attention to the act of rising and descending. The stairway at the Perry Street Loft, lit by a wall of fluorescent light, gives the ascension an otherworldly, perhaps even a heavenly, feel. And in the Pound Ridge House, with its stairways that rise alongside translucent fiberglass walls, inner and outer are subtly blurred, and the eye is free to wander both throughout the house and beyond it.

—

But it is the Hariris' rooms that I wanted to talk about. Getting to these roooms, in this essay as in the house themselves, is so interesting an experience that one is rightfully delayed. What engages me immediately in looking at these rooms is not so much what is there as what is *not* there. The eye is not stopped in these open spaces, and we are encouraged to notice, in Wallace Stevens's memorable phrase, "Nothing that is not there and the nothing that is." Sharp, clean lines, an abundance of free space, and an unspoken injunction against clutter that seems to inhere in the air itself, account for much of the distinctive feel of these rooms. But what is most distinctive about them is also what is most difficult to account for. All great art creates effects whose causes we cannot fully discern. Critics try, of course, and with mediocre works it is relatively easy to describe what is happening and why. One measure of a bad poet, for example, is that he can give you six reasons for every comma and line break. But before great works one feels a living presence that transcends the sum of its parts and resists interpretation.

—

It is difficult to uncover the source of the meditative stillness that seems to emanate from these rooms. But its effect is not only to create an aesthetically satisfying living space, but to release the mind from its attachment to form and guide it toward the invisible, shimmering realm of spirit. This conversation between the visible and invisible is given its fullest expression in the design for the Digital House with its walls made of liquid crystal displays that can mirror the passing skies, turn completely transparent, or display images to create the illusion of solidity. Here the boundary between inner and outer is truly porous, fluid and shifting. A more subtle and perhaps more soothing incarnation of the Hariris' spiritual and poetic impulses is manifested in the Greenwich House, which achieves a delicate balance between monastic simplicity and hearth-fire coziness. The living room flows into dining room and family room, and one feels that a breeze coming in any window would be free to circulate uninterrupted throughout the entire house. The Hariris describe the bedroom in the Greenwich House, with its fiberglass curtain wall that resembles a shoji screen, as "a place of solitude and dreams where one contemplates the interplay between being and nonbeing." And this is what I take Bachelard's statement to mean. The house must offer us a refuge and a release from the deadening conventions of reality that we are so rarely inclined to question. Waking and dreaming, openness and enclosure, inner and outer, being and nonbeing—these apparent dualities are subtly investigated, reversed, and sometimes merged in the Hariris' architecture.

—

Particularly in their masterful Sagaponac House, the interior spaces both express and invite an inner stillness. To live in these rooms must be a clarifying experience, an opportunity to empty the mind of its clutter and cultivate a mindfulness that would mirror the spaciousness of the rooms themselves. In the Sagaponac House, this interpenetration of inner and outer is enacted not only in the flowing free space of the house itself but also through the large floor-to-ceiling central windows that allow one to see into the soul of the house and indeed *through* the house to the surrounding woods on either side. Because of these windows and the L-shape of the design, one can view the exterior of the house from the interior and the interior from the exterior. This semi-transparency lets in as much as it keeps out, and the house itself becomes a metaphor for a receptive, nondualistic consciousness.

—

I am reminded, in looking at the Hariris' work, that the word "stanza," which in English designates a unit of verse, comes from an Italian word meaning "room." Which is strangely appropriate. With the greatest poems, one feels a desire not merely to read and think about them but to live *inside* them, a desire to leave one's prosaic surroundings, step into the poem, and take up residence within it. Living in one of the Hariris' houses would be one way to make that dream come true, to enter that unreality that is most real, to make of one's home a poem. And there is that syllable again: *home*, *om*, *poem*. One feels all three echoing in the spacious clarity of these rooms.

—

Project Credits

Sagaponac House:
Client: Harry "Coco" Brown
Architect: Hariri & Hariri—Architecture
Design Team: Gisue Hariri, Mojgan Hariri,
Thierry Pfister, Markus Randler
Structural Engineering: Robert Silman &
Associates, P.C.
Surveyor: Barylski Land Surveyor, P.C.
General Contractor: Ronan O'Dwyer
Photography: Paul Warchol (p 15, 17, 19,
20-21, 22-23, 25, 31, 32-33, 34, 36-37)
Francesca Giovanelli (p 24, 26, 27, 28, 29, 35)
Hariri & Hariri—Architecture (p18, 30)

Aqua House:
Client: Craig Robbins/Dacra Development
Corporation
Architect: Hariri & Hariri—Architecture
Design Team: Gisue Hariri, Mojgan Hariri,
Charles Jordan
Masterplan: Duany Plater-Zyberk & Company, Inc.
Executive Architects: Wolberg Alvarez &
Associates
Photography: Paul Warchol (p 41)
© Steven Brooke (p 39, 42-43, 45, 47, 48)
Renderings: Hariri & Hariri—Architecture

Park Avenue Loft:
Client: Gisue Hariri and Bahman Kia
Architecture and Interior Design: Hariri &
Hariri—Architecture
Design Team: Gisue Hariri, Mojgan Hariri,
Thierry Pfister, Markus Randler
General Contractor: Mark Chow
Millwork: Thornwood
Photography: Paul Warchol (p 54-55, 56-57,
59, 61, 64-65)
Åke Eson Lindman (p 51, 53, 58, 60, 62, 63)

Belmont House:
Client: Cheri Hariri and Paul Turner
Architect: Hariri & Hariri—Architecture
Design team: Gisue Hariri, Mojgan Hariri,
Marc Stierlin (Intern)
Civil Engineer: Robert Lyon
Structural Engineer: Martina Treister
Landscape Design: Keith Willig Landscape,
Architecture & Construction
General Contractor: Persicon
Metal Fabrication: Top Metal Design,
Redwood City, CA
Photography: Cesar Rubio

Perry Street Loft:
Client: Michael Aram
Architect: Hariri & Hariri—Architecture
Design Team: Gisue Hariri, Mojgan Hariri,
Thierry Pfister, Mason White (Intern)

Furniture and Accessories: Michael Aram
Structural Engineering: Robert Silman &
Associates, P.C.
Mechanical Engineering: Szekely Engineering
General Contractor: Fountainhead Construction
Photography: Paul Warchol (p 85, 87, 89,
90, 91)
Hariri & Hariri—Architecture (p 84, 88)

Pound Ridge House:
Client: Dr. Ihor and Barbara Cehelsky
Architect: Hariri & Hariri—Architecture
Design Team: Gisue Hariri, Mojgan Hariri,
Rika Onishi (Intern)
Structural Engineering: Ahneman
Associates, P.C.
General Contractor: Angelilli
Construction Corp.
Photography: Harry Zernike

The Digital House: The Un-Private House
Exhibition, MoMA, New York City, 1999–2000
Sponsor: *House Beautiful*
Architect: Hariri & Hariri—Architecture
Design team: Gisue Hariri, Mojgan Hariri,
Nadya Liebich, Marla Pasareno, Karin
Mousson (Interns)
Engineering: LCD Planar Optics,
Mark Borstelmann, Carl Gruderwald
Automation: Couture Technology,
Benjamin Rosner

Fifth Avenue Penthouse:
Client: Dale Ponikvar
Architect: Hariri & Hariri—Architecture
Design Team: Gisue Hariri, Mojgan Hariri,
Karin Mousson (Intern)
Structural Engineering: Robert Silman
Associates, P.C., Joe Tortorella
Mechanical: Szekely Engineering
General Contractor: Bernsohn & Fetner, LLC
Photography: Paul Warchol

Greenwich House:
Client: Ana and Esteban Nofal
Architect: Hariri & Hariri—Architecture
Design Team: Gisue Hariri, Mojgan Hariri,
Thierry Pfister (Intern)
Structural Engineer: Ahneman
Associates, P.C.
Consultant: Janice Parker—Landscape
General Contractor: GOL Construction, Inc.
Photography: Jason Schmidt

Riverbend House:
Client: K.B.F., Inc.
Architect: Hariri & Hariri—Architecture
Design Team: Gisue Hariri, Mojgan Hariri,
Graydon Yearick, Zoe Lin (Intern)
Structural Engineer: Robert Silman
Associates, P.C.

Surveying Engineer: Professional Design Group
General Contractor: Manco, Inc.
Photography: Jeff Goldberg

Spartan House:
Client: Geerlings Vastgoed B.V.
Architect: Hariri & Hariri—Architecture
Design Team: Gisue Hariri, Mojgan Hariri
(Principals in charge), Paul Baird, John
Bennett, Kristin Reuter (Intern)
Associate Architect: Versnel & Partners
Model Photography: Rick Scanlan
Photography: Ariel Huber

Barry's Bay Cottage:
Client: Jane Baird and Dr. Charles Baird
Architect: Hariri & Hariri—Architecture
Design Team: Gisue Hariri, Mojgan Hariri, Paul
Baird, Graydon Yearick, Brigid Hogan, Aaron
McDonald (Interns)
Structural Engineering: Robert Silman
Associates, P.C.
Surveyors: P. J. Stringer Surveying LTd.
General Contractor: Zuracon, Inc. (John
Lepinski, Mark Zuracowski)
Photography: John M. Hall

Villa The Hague:
Client: Geerlings Vastgoed B.V.
Architect: Hariri & Hariri—Architecture
Design Team: Gisue Hariri, Mojgan Hariri,
Paul Baird, Martha Skinner, Harry Zernike,
Aaron McDonald
Structural Engineering: Robert Silman
Associates, P.C.
Model Photography: Rick Scanlan

New Canaan House:
Client: Jeffrey and Donna Gorman
Architect: Hariri & Hariri—Architecture
Design Team: Gisue Hariri, Mojgan Hariri,
Andre Bideau, Yves Habegger, Kazem
Naderi, Paul Baird, William Wilson (Intern)
Structural Engineer: Ahneman
Associates, P.C.
General Contractor: GOL Construction
Photography: John M. Hall

Soho Loft:
Client: Kathleen Schneider
Architects: Hariri & Hariri—Architecture
Design Team: Gisue Hariri, Mojgan Hariri,
Andre Bideau (Intern)
General Contractor: Marko Tomich, Inc.
Metal Fabrication: Dan George, Mark Gibian
Photography: John. M. Hall

Selected Bibliography

Books

Asensio, Paco. *Mountain Houses*. New York: HarperCollins, 2000.

Brown, Harry J. *American Dream: The Houses at Sagaponac*. New York: Rizzoli International Publications, 2003.

Christiaanse, Kees, and Hans Ibelings. *STRIP: One Mile of Urban Planning in The Hague*. Rotterdam: NAi Publishers, 2003.

Doubilet, Susan, and Daralice Boles. *American House Now: Contemporary Architectural Directions*. New York: Universe Publishing, 1997.

Images Publishing Group. *Office Spaces: A Pictorial Review*. Australia: Images Publishing Group Pty. Ltd., 2003.

Lang Ho, Cathy, and Raul A. Barreneche. *House: American Houses for the New Century*. New York: Universe Publishing, 2001.

Mostadi, Arian. *The American House Today*. Barcelona, Spain: Architecture Showcase, 2000.

Phillips, Patricia. *Bearings: Faculty Architecture in North America*. Parsons School of Design, ex. cat. New York: Princeton Architectural Press, 1988–89.

Protetch, Max, and Stuart Krimko. *A New World Trade Center: Design Proposals from Leading Architects Worldwide*. New York: Regan Books, 2002.

Reschke, Cynthia. *Pacific Houses*. New York: Harper Design International, 2004.

Richards, Ivor. *Manhattan Lofts*. London: John Wiley & Sons, 2000.

Riera Ojeda, Oscar. *Hariri & Hariri: Work in Progress*. New York: Monacelli, 1995.

———. *The New American House*. New York: Whitney Library of Design, 1995.

Riley, Terence. *The Un-Private House*. New York: Museum of Modern Art, 1999.

Russel, Beverly. *40 Under 40: A Guide to New Young Talents with Seductive Ideas for Living Today*. Vitae Publishing Inc., 1995.

Sirefman, Susanna. *New York: A Guide to Recent Architecture*." Ellipsis Konemann, 1997.

Smith Brownstein, Elizabeth. *If This House Could Talk . . . .* New York: Simon & Schuster, 1999.

Toy, Maggie. *The Architect: Woman in Contemporary Architecture*. Australia: Images Publishing Group Pty. Ltd., 2001

Trulove, James Grayson, and Il Kim. *The New American House 3: Innovations in Residential Design and Construction*. New York: Whitney Library of Design, 2001.

———. *The New American House 4: Innovations in Residential Design and Construction*. New York: Whitney Library of Design, 2001.

Periodicals

Abramovitch, Ingrid. "American Scene—This Month on the Design Beat." *House & Garden*, January 2005, p. 45.

"The AD 100: The World's Top Designers and Architects." *Architectural Digest*, January 2004, p. 80.

The American Institute of Architecture, New York Chapter. "Hariri & Hariri: Rockland Center for the Arts." *Oculus*, vol. 63, no. 6, February 2001, p. 5.

"Architecture." *Zoo*, no. 5, April 2000, p. 121.

Bernstein, Fred. "From Industrial Relic to Brave New World: The High Line Gets a Second Chance." *Architectural Record*, October 2003, pp. 73–74.

———. "Top of the Line." *Surface*, no. 43, August 2003, pp. 162–170.

———. "Renovate." *Metropolitan Home*, September/October 1999, pp. 163–171.

———. "Comforts of Modern." Edited by Linda O'Keefe. *Metropolitan Home*, September/October 1997, pp. 132–141.

Bierman, Lindsay. "Sister Act," ed. Elizabeth Sverbeyeff Byron. *Elle Decor*, October/November 1995, pp. 268–273.

"Cincinnati Exhibition of Dream Houses." *Architecture*, January 1994, pp. 27–29.

Colman, David. "On a Curve." *Elle Decor*, March 2005, pp. 102–107.

"DMZ." Storefront for Art and Architecture exhibition catalogue, *Front 3*, November 1988, p. 60.

Filler, Martin. "Two Part Harmony." *House Beautiful*, February 1999, pp. 96–101.

———. "User Friendly." *House Beautiful*, November 1994, pp. 114–117.

Ford, Jen. "The House of Tomorrow." *Harper's Bazaar*, October 2004, pp. 192–193.

Frampton, Kenneth. "Criticism: On the Work of Hariri & Hariri." *A+U*, July 1993, pp. 81–130.

Frankel, Elena. "Speaking Volumes" *Interior Design*, vol. 71, no. 2, February 2000, pp. 146–153.

———. "Suburban Urbanism." *Interior Design*, vol. 62, no. 5, May 1999, pp. 292–299.

———. "Making a Spec House Special." *Architectural Record*, Record Houses, April 1998, pp. 68–75.

Freiman, Ziva. "Young Architects." *PA*, July 1990, pp. 64–65.

"Futures to Come." *Architectural Record*, December 1999, pp. 100–101.

Gandee, Charles. "The Young Contenders." *HG*, August 1988, pp. 86–92.

Gardiner, Virginia. "Seeing What Develops." *Dwell*, June 2005, pp. 130–135.

Geibel, Victoria. "Material Witness." *Architecture*, June 1990, pp. 64–67.

Goldberger, Paul. "Homes of the Stars." *New Yorker*, September 13, 2004, pp. 96–99.

Goodman, Wendy. "Urban Oasis." *New York Magazine*, October 14, 2002, pp. 42–45.

———. "Home Design 2000." *New York Magazine*, October 11, 1999, pp. 72–77.

———. "The Digital Habitat." *Harper's Bazaar*, September 1995, pp. 346–352.

Gordon, Alastair. "37 Ways of Looking at a Hampton." *Vanity Fair*, May 2003, pp. 198–199.

"Gorman Residence." *GA Houses 31*, Project 1991, pp. 94–95.

Hall, John. "Sisters in the Ascendant." *The World of Interiors*, December 1989, pp. 44–47.

Hamilton, William L. "Critic's Choice." *Metropolitan Home*, January/February 1993, pp. 20–23.

Iovine, Julie V. "Sibling Revelry." *Metropolitan Home*, August 1990, pp. 138–140.

Jacobs, Karrie. "Sub-Minimal Message." *New York Magazine*, February 24, 1997.

"JSM Music Studios." Environments I.D. Award, *I.D.*, July/August 1993, p. 139.

"Juan Valdez Café." *New York Magazine*, October 18, 2004, p. 60.

"Kash Villa." *GA Houses 34*, Project 1992, pp. 31–33.

Leish Brown, Patricia. "Double Identity." *Architectural Digest*, May 2003, pp. 300–305.

Loukin, Andrea. "Hariri & Hariri." *Interior Design*, March 1994, pp. 8–11.

———. "Hariri & Hariri." *Interior Design*, July 1994, pp. 101–103, 148–149.

Makovsky, Paul, and Andrew Yang. "The Twenty-First-Century Coffee Shop." *Metropolis*, March 2005, p.118.

Mellins, Thomas. "The Gap Between the Promise and the Prototype." *Architectural Record*, July 2003, pp. 74–80.

Merkel, Jayne. "Reaching Out." *Oculus*, The America Institute of Architects, vol. 57, no. 9, May 1995, pp. 10–11.

"Modern Dream." *New York Times Homes* section, July 2004, cover and p. 2.

Moseley, Amanda. "Read Me." *Metropolis*, April 2005, p. 42.

Pearson, Clifford A. "Canadian Au Pair." *Architectural Record: Record Houses*, April 1995, pp. 96–101.

———. "Sum of Its Parts." *Architectural Record: Record Houses*, April 1993, p. 76–83.

"Relative Merits." *Wallpaper*, February 1999, p. 72.

Renzi, Jen. "Showing Off." *Interior Design*, February 2002, pp. 188–190.

Riera Ojeda, Oscar. "Hariri & Hariri." *Casas International*, no. 48. Argentina: Kliczkowski, April 1997.

Russel, Beverly. "40 Under 40." *Interiors*, September 1995, p. 68.

Schoeneman, Deborah. "Gems of the Ocean." *New York Magazine*, November 15, 2004, p. 78.

Sforni, Jasmine. "Dressed To Thrill." *Surface*, no. 52, p. 86.

Stephens, Suzanne. "To the Lighthouse Creatively." *New York Times*, November 24, 1988, p. C3.

Tonkinson, Carole. "The Greatful Bed." *Elle Decor*, April/May 1993, p. 64.

Vogel, Carol. "Material Matters." *New York Times Magazine*, January 6, 1991, pp. 48–49.

Webb, Michael. "Caffeine H(e)aven." *Frame*, January/February 2005, p. 40.

Zevon, Susan. "Pushing the Digital Envelope." *House Beautiful*, "Houses of the Next Millennium" series, October 1998, pp. 66–70.

Awards

The American Academy of Arts and Letters, Academy Award in Architecture, 2005

Hospitality Design First Annual Awards for Creative Achievement, Hospitality Debut Award, 2005

The AD 100: The World's Top Designers and Architects Award, 2004

St. Mark's Coptic Canadian Village, International Design Competition for a Master Plan, 2004

Designing the High Line, Ideas Competition, honorable mention and selected entry for exhibition at Grand Central Terminal, 2003

The City's 100 Best Architects, *New York Magazine*, 2002

Saatchi & Saatchi Award, Finalist for Innovation and Communication, 2000

The School of Visual Arts, New York, 40 Under 40 Award, 1996

Architectural Record, Record Houses, Award 1995

The Architectural League of New York, Emerging Voice Award, 1995

IX Bienal Panamericana de Arquitectura Award, 1994

ID Annual Design Review Award, 1993

Builder's Choice, Design & Planning Awards, 1993
Grand Award for Private Residence (New Canaan House)

Architectural Record, Record Houses Award, 1993

Progressive Architecture, Young Architects Award, 1990

The Architectural League of New York, Young Architects Forum Award, 1990

Exhibitions

2005

Pratt Manhattan Gallery
New York, NY
Record Houses

The American Academy of Arts and Letters
New York, NY
Exhibition of Works by Newly Elected
Members and Recipients of Honors and Awards

Seaport World Trade Center
Boston, MA
Record Houses

Triennale di Milano
Milan, Italy
Dressing Ourselves

2004

National Building Museum
Washington, D.C.
Liquid Stone: New Architecture in Concrete

2003

Grand Central Terminal
New York, NY
Designing the High Line

Dansk Arkitektur Center
Copenhagen, Denmark
Futures to Come

Deutsches Arkitektur Museum
Frankfurt, Germany
A New World Trade Center: Design Proposals

Galeria Ferran Cano
Mallorca, Spain
I Love New York

2002

CUBE Centre
Manchester, UK
A New World Trade Center: Design Proposals

Galeria Ferran Cano
Barcelona, Spain
I Love New York

8th Biennale of Architecture in Venice
Venice, Italy
A New World Trade Center: Design Proposals

National Building Museum
Washington, D.C.
A New World Trade Center: Design Proposals

Max Protetch Gallery
New York, NY
A New World Trade Center: Design Proposals

2001

Museu d'Art Contemporani de Barcelona
Barcelona, Spain
Barcelona Art Report 2001 Triennial

2000

Armand Hammer Museum at UCLA
Los Angeles, CA

The Un-Private House

The Walker Art Center
Minneapolis, MN
The Un-Private House

Austrian Museum of Applied Arts
Vienna, Austria
The Un-Private House

SCI-Arc
Los Angeles, CA
Second International Architectural Exhibit
and Auction March 2000

Hamburger Architektur Sommer 2000
Hamburg, Germany
Women and Xtended Visions

Berkeley Art Museum
Berkeley, CA
2 x 2: Architectural Collaboration

1999

Max Protetch Gallery
New York, NY
Futures to Come

GLASGOW 1999
Glasgow, UK
The Digital House

The Museum of Modern Art
New York, NY
The Un-Private House

1996

Robert Lehman Gallery at Urban Glass Center
Brooklyn, NY
House for The Next Millennium

1995

AIA Baltimore
Six Houses

1994

The Parrish Art Museum
South Hampton, NY
The Second Parrish Art Museum Design
Biennial: Mirrors

D&D Building
New York, NY
Fantasy Chair Exhibit

1993

University of Houston
Houston, TX
City, Room, Garden

Texas A&M University
College Station, TX
City, Room, Garden

SCI-Arc
Los Angeles, CA
International Architectural Exhibition and Sale
(Scholarship Fundraiser)

The Contemporary Arts Center
Cincinnati, OH
The Architect's Dream: Houses for the Next

Millennium

Cornell University
Ithaca, NY
Female Construct

Richard Anderson Gallery
New York, NY
Curated by Nancy Spiro
"It is a matter of force. Tension . . . Compression."

1991

Kent State University
Kent, OH
Hariri & Hariri *Catharsis*

1990

The Architectural League of New York
New York, NY
Young Architects Forum 1990

1988

Princeton University
Princeton, NJ
Selected Work

Parsons School of Design
New York, NY
Bearings: Faculty Architecture in North
America

Storefront for Art and Architecture
New York, NY
Project DMZ

Lighthouse Donation
New York, NY
Lighthouse Development Center
Auction at Tiffany & Co.
Exhibition & Preview at D&D Building

1987

Alliance in the Park
Philadelphia, PA
An Outdoor/Indoor Exhibition of
Collaborative Works

Milan Triennale
Milan, Italy
Urban Design Exhibition

1986

Equilibrium Project

Via New York
Mexico City, Mexico
Architectural Exhibition
Other Participants: Zaha Hadid, Rem
Koolhaas, Steven Holl, Lebbeus Woods,
Giuliano Fiorenzoli, Andrew McNair

1982

Philippe Bonnafont Gallery
San Francisco, CA
Architectural Drawings

1980

Cornell University
Ithaca, NY
Dutch Facades

Acknowledgments

This book would not have been possible without the commitment of Charles Miers, David Morton, Ron Broadhurst, and Julie Di Filippo of Rizzoli International Publications. I am grateful for their understanding, advice, and willingness to make this book a reality.

—

Claudia Brandenburg brought her remarkable skill and imagination to the design of this book. I admire her talent, appreciate her professionalism, and I am thankful to her for making the long process of creating this book such a pleasure.

—

I am also grateful to my associate Markus Randler for making "everything" he works on very special, including his tireless effort in gathering the material for this book.

—

Architecture is impossible without the drive, dedication, and will to continue in spite of all hardship and disappointments. Many interns, designers, and associates have put their minds and hearts into the projects selected for this book. I am thankful to all of them but especially to Thierry Pfister and Markus Randler, whose dedication, talent, hard work, and love of architecture make them a vitally important part of Hariri & Hariri Architecture.

—

We are extremely thankful to Paul Goldberger, Richard Meier, and John Brehm for their long-standing support of our work and for contributing such elegant and insightful essays to this book. They have each inspired, educated, and helped us grow during the past twenty years.

—

We are grateful to our clients, who have trusted our decisions and have given us the opportunity to explore beyond comfortable norms, and to the many contractors, craftsmen, and artisans who have helped us to realize our work in the past twenty years. Here we would particularly like to acknowledge Marko Tomich, Steve Fetner, Frank Afshari, Dan George, Mark Gibian, Scott Madison, and John Kern for their continuous efforts to maintain the highest standards.

—

We are extremely thankful to the photographers who have captured the essence of our work so artfully. We are grateful in particular to Paul Warchol, Jason Schmidt, Jeff Goldberg, Cesar Rubio, Harry Zernike, Francesca Giovanelli, Ake Eson Lindman, Ariel Huber, Rick Scanlan, John Hall, Steven Brooke, and Luca Vignelli.

—

Our final thanks are to our family and friends for their generous support during the best and worst of times and for never losing confidence in our vision. We would particularly like to thank Karim and Behjat Hariri, Cheri Hariri, Paul Turner, Bahman Kia, and Iman and Ava Hariri-Kia.

—